Aun Cookbook

A Man's Cooking

by Joe Sears

*In Pearl's kitchen on the front cover,
can you find:*

The handmade Aunt Pearl cookie jar
A bottle of strychnine for "bitter pills"
Pearl's Native American sweetgrass
Opal's prize eggs?

Published by Pearl Productions
1991

**This book is dedicated to
Dolly May, June, Jean and Biddy**

Aunt Pearl's Cookbook was inspired from the characters created by Jaston Williams, Joe Sears and Ed Howard in their stage play series of *Greater Tuna, A Tuna Christmas,* and *Red, White and Tuna.*

To order copies of *Aunt Pearl's Cookbook* use order form in the back of this book or write directly to:

Pearl Productions
P.O. Box 49301
Austin, Texas 78765

Printed by Morgan Printing, Austin, Texas.

Cover photo: © Scott Newton, Austin, Texas, 1991.

ISBN 0-9631606-0-5

INTRODUCTION

As you can see from thumbing through this cookbook, there are no short-cuts on calories or fat. My cooking is designed to keep a man happy, since that is the way we girls were raised. Our secret to good cooking is good loving from the men who eat our dishes. Most of these recipes require a little time, but they're special and some only appear at holidays, reunions and funerals.

Some of the recipes are from the residents of Tuna, Texas. Other recipes are from the real world, but all the recipes are legitimate. Featured inside are four cooks who stand above the rest in our family: our head cook, Biddy, Dolly May, June and Jean. When I lay out a country dinner, I thank these cooks. There are a few secret recipes included here, well, not secret after this printing, but protected until now. One should be thankful and take advantage of learning them.

It used to be a "woman thing" to watch the menfolk line up for our food at special gatherings, and what they lined up for is right here in this cookbook. Most of the recipes are from country cooks on farms and ranches, but there are a few from city folks too. There are also a few recipes from men scattered about inside and that's because some "man cooks" have indeed achieved what women made an art.

In this book I refer to "Opal's eggs". She is not a competitor in my egg business, but rather my best laying hen. Opal lays the best tasting eggs I've ever eaten and I use her eggs in all my cooking. I never sell her eggs. Opal got her name one day when she swallowed a valuable opal setting I received from my first husband. I saw the setting fly off my ring and Opal was quick to eat it. She's never passed the opal, 'cause I check every "passing". I can't eat her, not my best layer, but I know that jewel is inside of her somewhere. I keep Opal close at hand and check all her eggs as I use them, just in case that setting miraculously slips inside.

The profits from this cookbook are being donated to AIDS Research in hopes and prayers that this "killing" will stop. Too many men and women have "left" their family gatherings to be celebrated without them, and as you know, most of these men and women were cut down before their prime. On behalf of all those mothers who miss their children at the table, we dedicate our efforts.

Pearl Burras

CONTENTS

VEGETABLES & SIDE DISHES

BREADS & SWEETS

SPECIAL OCCASIONS

Photo by Burdette Parks

Pearl's Family and Friends.
Top row left to right: My grandnephew Stanley, his awful father Hank, Vera Carp, me, my niece Bertha.
Bottom row left to right: Thurston Wheelis and Arlis Struvie (disc jockeys of OKKK), my grandniece Charlene, Jody and his dogs (Dolly and Blossom), Reverend Spikes at far right.

HOLIDAY TURKEY
Texas

Cooking a turkey is not hard and this old-fashioned recipe will give you that Grandma taste and Aunt Pearl smell for a traditional Holiday offering. I cook turkey at Thanksgiving and Christmas and not at any other time of the year, making this feast something the family always looks forward to.

Turkey
Margarine, at room temperature
Salt and Pepper
2 large onions, quartered
Stalk of celery with top leaves, cut in large pieces
2 cups water
Small bowl of water and flour mixed together for
    a thick, creamy texture.

Thaw any size turkey. Wash it down real good in the sink and don't be ashamed of scrubbing her down good. Make the old girl sing like Ethel Merman. My kids lived for this event each year as all my turkeys sang in the shower as if their forthcoming debut was at Town Hall. This bird you're washing is the star of the show and should be treated as such. You'll have more fun watching the turkey bathe if you select a noted singer. I've cooked several Ethel Merman turkeys and a Kate Smith or two and I remember one Billie Holiday bird.

Slightly dry Ethel with paper towels. Grab a handful of margarine and rub it between your hands. Now rub the star as if she's getting her final massage. Make sure you get plenty of margarine rubbed into the bird. Now, with margarine still on your hands, rub a palmful of salt between your hands and apply this to the bird as you did the margarine, making sure plenty of salt gets rubbed in. You need not worry about too much salt or margarine and a couple of handfuls may be required.

Lightly pepper the bird, but don't rub this in. Dip your hands in the creamy paste created from the watered down "kid's paste" of flour and water. Dab this lightly on the skin, careful not to go over areas already covered with paste. This is not a crust, but a more delicious sealer.

Place turkey in a large roasting pan. Place quartered onions under wings behind drumsticks, in the cavity, and some on the bottom of the pan to cook in the broth that you'll need later on. Now place the celery alongside the onion and leave the celery tops in the bottom of the pan to cook in the broth.

Pour 2 cups of cool water in bottom of pan. Do not pour over turkey. Preheat oven to 350° and let the bird cook slow. Cover and cook the turkey for at least a couple of hours or until the meat turns brown and falls apart at the limbs. This is a tender turkey and will not hold up to carving at the table. Prepare your turkey platter on the kitchen cabinet as this bird will fall apart if you try and lift it.

After the turkey has cooked for at least 1½ hours, baste the turkey every 30 minutes. Drain off broth to use for noodles and stuffing. Serve with Aunt Biddie's Noodles and Norma's Cornbread Stuffing (recipes in this book).

EASTER HAM
Texas

This is a traditional meal after Easter church service and the ham needs to be as pretty and bright as the eggs hidden in the backyard. My hams are pretty and brown and have an old-fashioned taste.

8 to 12 lb. lean ham
Aluminum foil
Whole cloves
Ringed pineapple slices
Apricot glaze (see recipe below)

Cover a roasting pan with a large sheet of aluminum foil. Place ham in the center, smooth half of the apricot glaze over the ham at this time.. Bring foil up over ham and cover loosely. Bake at 375° for 3 hours.

Remove ham after 3 hours and cut off rind (fat). Score lines in a pattern across the ham making sure each square has a clove in the center. Now brush on remaining apricot glaze and place pineapples over ham. Use cloves as toothpicks to secure things. Cook 1 more hour, uncovered. Baste from time to time during this last hour.

Pearl's Apricot Glaze

1 cup honey
1 cup or jar of apricot jam
Grated peel of ½ an orange
2 tsp. cider vinegar

Mix all together adding cider vinegar if too thick. Spoon over ham 35 minutes before serving.

PEARL'S SUPERBOWL CHILI
Texas

This is my most popular recipe. It's great for Saturday picnics with hotdogs, or Frito pies and especially on Superbowl Sundays when I serve it to my husband during the game. He likes it with plain ol' saltine crackers and with onions and cheese on top. I like to eat mine on a hot dog at a cookout. The gathering will love you for your efforts. I always cook a big pot so there will be individual servings to freeze for later on in the winter or at the next summer cookout.

    4 lbs. lean hamburger meat
    1 large yellow onion, finely chopped
    1 bell pepper, finely chopped
    1 large can of tomato juice, largest can on shelf
    1 pkg. chili seasoning mix (Any commercial brand will
       do. I have used many varieties and have never been
       displeased.)

Brown meat, bell pepper and onion in a pot, seasoning with salt and pepper. Drain off fat, return to the heat and add chili seasoning mix, stirring in well. Now pour half of the tomato juice into the pot and stir awhile before adding remainder of tomato juice. Bring to a boil, then reduce heat to a simmer and cook for 1½ hours, stirring often.

EARL'S PICNIC
Oklahoma

Earl selects a secluded and romantic cove each year on beautiful Lake Tenkiller for his annual picnic. Being a romantic, he makes sure that everything is just right. If one small thing goes wrong, Earl might stomp out the fire, grab the fishing poles and head for home. Knowing this, his guests hold their breath each year and hope that nothing will go wrong. The truth is, Earl has never failed to produce a flawless picnic. Earl begins his picnic three hours before dusk and ends it just as the June moon rises over the lake. Here's Earl's own description.

Earl's Salad

"Soup and salad are the really civilized rudiments of good picnicking. These, with the addition of a good loaf of crusty bread, some fresh fruit (pears, apples, melons, or grapes), and a healthy chunk of Brie, can only be enhanced by a bottle of Sutter Home White Zinfandel.

"My favorite salad, and one which I have served Pearl Burras on several summer occasions, is a layered concoction made from whatever is freshest and prettiest in one of my neighbors' gardens. I usually begin with a large clear glass bowl so the colors of each can really shine. Then I arrange at least seven or more of the following in layers. Each time a new layer is complete, be certain to press gently but firmly on top. This salad must be well packed."

> 2 cups finely torn lettuce
> 1 cup tomatoes, seeded and chopped
> 1 cup thinly sliced
>   radishes
> 1 cup red onion rings
> ½ cup coarsely chopped
>   bell pepper
> 1 cup grated Monterey
>   Jack cheese
> 1 cup drained, canned
>   red beans
> 1 cup thawed and
>   drained frozen green peas
> 1 cup thinly sliced pepperoni
> ½ cup coarsely chopped celery
> 1 cup cucumber, peeled and sliced thin
> 2 cups finely torn fresh spinach
> ½ cup drained canned mushrooms
> 1 cup canned shoepeg corn, drained

"After you have arranged your layers in a suitable color scheme, press down firmly, then top with ¼ inch of homemade mayonnaise, to which you've added a little garlic for surprise. Chill overnight. This is a must! This salad cannot be hurried. Just before serving, garnish with chopped black olives and freshly crumbled bacon. A good accompaniment is soup, such as the chilled raspberry soup below."

Earl's Chilled Raspberry Soup

> 1 pkg. frozen raspberries
> 1 apple, peeled and seeded
> ½ cup frozen orange juice concentrate
> 1 cup red wine
> Juice of 1 lemon
> 2 cups water
> Sugar

"In a blender combine raspberries, apple, orange juice, wine, lemon juice and water. Blend until smooth. Sweeten with sugar or artificial sweetener if desired. Store in the blender until ready to serve. I prefer serving it in chilled bowls with a garnish of vanilla yogurt, a sprig of fresh mint, a lemon peel curl and a couple of whole raspberries. If, when ready to serve, it is too thick, add several ice cubes and blend again; if it's still too thick, add a small can of water before blending.

"I took this soup to a Bumiller reunion once. Being Baptists, they took a hearty objection to the wine. I told them to try making it with white grape juice. They now serve it at all social functions. Pearl assures me they make it with wine and simply tell everybody it's grape juice - much like the Methodists do at communion."

C. K.'S TAOS FRUIT SALAD
New Mexico

I know a gaggle of women out there who can lay out some fine cooking, but C. K.'s fruit salad is my favorite. It's made with fresh seasoned and exotic fruits for a taste to make you stay longer in Taos and "blow-off" that visit to the Santa Fe Opera.

    2 bananas
    1 papaya
    2 apples
    2 pears
    1 pint strawberries
    ½ lb. or less red grapes
    ¼ tsp. vanilla
    ¼ tsp. nutmeg
    Vanilla yogurt (1 container)

Cut fruit to bite size pieces and mix all together, sprinkle with nutmeg. Mix in the vanilla yogurt and the vanilla extract. Chill slightly before serving.

PEARL'S SUNDAY POT ROAST
Texas

This American classic is prepared in many ways, some too modern for my tastes. To retain the old-fashioned flavors, don't try this in a microwave. This recipe will make that little boy in your husband pop out after eating it. It's cooked to fork tenderness, as it was originally intended. My first husband would hold my hand all day after I served this.

Any lean roast
2 large Russet Potatoes, split in half
4 carrots, medium-sized
½ head cabbage
Bacon grease
Flour
Onions
Water
Salt and pepper

Use a dutch oven skillet or a large roasting pan. Cook seasoned, floured meat in bacon grease until all sides have been browned. Reduce heat and add the onions to the pan and brown meat one more time quickly with the onions. Now pour 2 cups of water into the pan, cover and cook at 350° for 1 hour.

Reduce heat to 325° and let cook another hour. Add potatoes, carrots, and quartered cabbage half around the meat in the juice. Cook another hour, serve hot. If your meat is fork tender after 2 hours, add vegetables and only cook until the vegetables are done.

ENOCH'S CATFISH QUARTBULLION
"COOBY-YON"
aka Catfish Soup
Louisiana

Enoch's Cafe is one of those places you can count on for several good things. Good music and good food are the headliners. Musicians love this Louisiana stop and more than one Texas picker has had to call home and tell the Ms. that he'll be late one more night. Doyle Jeter, proprietor of Enoch's, shares this true Cajun delight.

Use fresh ingredients!
4 cups water
3 lbs. catfish fillets
¾ cup olive oil
2 green bell peppers
1 large white onion
Handful of celery
3 fresh tomatoes, crushed
3 cloves fresh chopped garlic
3 10-ounce cans of tomato sauce
Spices: Dash of filé powder, oregano, red cayenne,
   black pepper, sweet basil, thyme, rosemary
2 T. sugar
2 T. garlic powder
3 bay leaves
Salt to taste
Parsley, for garnish
Chopped green onion, for garnish
Cooked rice

Bring water to a boil in a large gumbo pot. Put in catfish fillet. In a separate pan, heat olive oil and saute bell pepper, onion, celery, tomato and chopped garlic. When catfish is to the point of falling apart (which it will do naturally), add the sauteed vegetables to the catfish. At this point, add the rest of the spices, cans of tomato sauce, sugar, salt, etc. Simmer for one hour and serve over rice. Garnish with fresh parsley and chopped green onions. Serve with French bread and lots of cold Dixie beer. Serves a bunch of folks or two members of Gary P. Nunn's Sons of the Bunkhouse Band.

JOHN'S BACKYARD BRISKET
Oklahoma

John cooks for Yellowstone National Park in the summers and doesn't have time to do this brisket, so he cooks it a lot in the fall and winter making this brisket very popular for the Holidays. He uses a regular patio smoker with layers for water and charcoal. To get John's tender smoked brisket you must pay close attention to his steaming secret at the end of the cooking. Guaranteed results.

> **8 to 10 lb. brisket**
> **Garlic powder**
> **Water**
> **Charcoal smoker with a temperature gauge**

Dust brisket evenly with garlic powder and put in smoker at ideal heat, 350°. About every hour stir coals up and add a couple chunks of hickory to the coals as you stir. Smoke meat for 10 to 11 hours then put brisket in a closed pan or roaster and add a quart of water to the bottom. Bake covered in the oven at 300° for about an hour to help steam the meat. Add more water if necessary to keep from burning. Take out and drain, trimming off the fat. Slice thin for sandwiches.

MAIN DISHES

Photo by Scott Newton

JUNE'S FRIED CHICKEN
Oklahoma

June is one of those cooks whose name is associated with the best of country cooking. If food is the focus, this woman is there with an easy-going attitude and a dish folks will stand in line for. Her country fried chicken is out of this world and below are her secrets to this Sunday meal favorite.

Electric skillet
Cut up chicken
Crisco shortening
Flour
Salt and pepper

Wash chicken in cold water. Salt chicken real well. (June says it's okay to over-salt because much of it will cook off, and this chicken is not salted after it's fried. I'm convinced that over-salting is one of her secrets.) While chicken is wet and salted, slightly pepper the pieces. Now roll them very lightly in flour, not pressing flour to the skin. June barely touches the piece, yet each piece is covered with flour.

Melt the Crisco in electric skillet and set on a medium-high position. You want this grease to be hot but not too hot when you begin. Grease should be half way up the sides of the skillet. Place chicken all around the skillet not overlapping any pieces. Grease should be hot enough to sizzle when the pieces are placed in the pan. Cover and cook for 12 minutes without checking or turning. If the grease is too hot, reduce heat. Chicken should be turned only once when sides of the chicken have turned brown. After turning the chicken you may move some pieces around. Cover this and cook for another 10 minutes or until the chicken is tender.

If the drumstick shows the bone shaft near the bottom of the piece, you'll know the piece is done. June says not to put any new pieces in the fry pan until all of the first batch have finished. Drain on paper towels. Serve with Red Eye Gravy and mashed potatoes, June's Corn on the Cob and Earl's Salad.

ROB'S CHICKEN
Chicken and Mustard Sauce with Glazed Apples
New York

When I can stand it, New York is always a lot of fun even if you have to take the God-awful subway. Getting out to dine is an art form in New York, but the best cooking is done by New Yorkers at home. Rob is a lawyer and serves this chicken delight at his lower "Soho" loft apartment. He recommends Far Niete Chardonnay, Napa Valley, as the wine to serve with this dish. It's $28 a bottle but that's New Yorkers for you.

> **4 chicken breasts**
> **Seasoned bread crumbs**
> **2 jars of Dijon Mustard**
> **3 eggs**
> **White wine**
> **Cooking oil**
> **4 apples**
> **Sugar**
> **Butter**

Marinate chicken breasts in Dijon mustard and 3 eggs from one hour to overnight (in the refrigerator). Heat oil in pan over medium to low heat. Coat chicken with bread crumbs - pack crumbs onto chicken. Brown chicken in oil, about 1 minute on each side, then cook for 20 minutes in a 350° oven.

Sauce
Add wine to mustard. Slice apples and brown them in butter and sugar. Pour mustard sauce and apples over chicken when cooked.

HEN AND DRESSING
Arkansas

Virginia Floyd is a Fort Smith cook who means business when she says, "Now Pearl, this is not turkey and dressing, its hen and dressing." And you best do what she says or one of her big strapping boys will show up on your doorstep to defend Mama's recipe. Virginia's hen and dressing is perfect for a newlywed to learn and once this "Sunday tradition" is mastered you can look forward to a marriage lasting as long as Arkansas.

Virginia: "This makes enough to feed a large family gathering or church pot-luck. I use a hen for dressing even if I'm cooking turkey."

5 to 6 lb. roasting hen
1 whole stalk of celery, tops included (about 3 cups)
2 large onions
1 recipe of cornbread, crumbled
4 to 5 cups of crumbled light bread, rolls or biscuits
4 eggs, slightly beaten
3 tsp. parsley flakes
1 tsp. salt
½ tsp. pepper
1 tsp. sugar
½ tsp. celery seeds
1 tsp. onion salt
3 tsp. rubbed sage
½ tsp. garlic powder

The day before: Make corn bread (Virginia says to make plenty in a 12 inch iron skillet. It smells so good baking, she has a slice with sweet milk when it comes out of the oven.) Cook the hen in plenty of water (with no seasoning) until meat falls off the bone. When cool, strip the meat from the bone and throw away the skin. Store meat and broth separately. Should make about 3 quarts of broth.

Cooking day: Heat broth while mixing remaining ingredients. Mix the breads in the large roasting pan in which dressing will be baked. Mix in coarsely chopped onion and celery. Add seasonings. Add eggs by hand. Add hot broth and bake at 350° for 45 minutes. At this time, stir in the chicken meat, mixing well, bake another 45 minutes to 1 hour. If it gets too dry on top, add boiling water over it. (Don't let it get too dry.)

PEARL'S CHICKEN SOUP
Texas

Out West they catch big colds and in New York they sneeze all winter. Down South we just eat this soup and it keeps the mosquitoes away. Chicken soup is known as the "Jewish Penicillin" and it works on the biggest of men. If you're not counting calories, this makes a filling dinner soup. If you're after a cold, make sure you use large onions. Onions are essential in this soup; don't be afraid to use all five.

    5 lb. chicken, cut up
    4 quarts water
    1 bunch celery with tops, chopped
    5 medium onions, chopped
    5 sprigs parsley, chopped
    3 tsp. salt
    ½ to 1 tsp. pepper

Salt chicken well before cooking, then add pepper. In a large pot, cook chicken, onions, celery and parsley at a boil until chicken falls off the bone (about 2 hours). Drain all the contents. Strip chicken from bone and return the meat to the soup pot. Also return the onions and celery in any amount desired. Reheat. Mix a smooth paste of flour with chicken broth. Mix this into the soup and cook on medium for another 30 minutes. Add steamed rice and serve.

CHICKEN LIVER OMELETTE
Alabama

This is a chicken liver lovers delight. I first ate this omelette in Alabama where they know many recipes for chicken liver. This Alabama recipe is sauted in butter and flavored with Tony Chachere's Famous Creole Seasoning. Serve with homefried potatoes.

Chicken livers
1 small onion, chopped
¼ stick butter
Tony Chachere's Famous Creole Seasoning
2 eggs

Wash and drain livers. In a saucepan melt ¼ stick of butter. Season livers well with Tony Chachere's and place in butter over low heat. Sprinkle onion over pieces of meat. Saute until livers are well done. Use as a filling for the omelette.

SAN FRANCISCO CHICKEN SALAD
California

I had slipped on a Nob Hill sidewalk and rolled half a block before two Chinese boy's stopped me, helped me up and suggested I take the cable car. I took their advice and boarded a car down to Post Street where I got off and had lunch at the "Post Street Cafe." I've never regretted going through their doors and on many visits there I've ordered the "Post Street Chicken Salad". I never had the nerve to ask for the recipe, so I tried to memorize it and have had 100% results in taste. I can't call it "Post Street Chicken Salad" but suggest you eat it there on a future visit. Until then, here's a great "close enough". I've turned heads at many a brunch or club meeting with this salad. I took it to Joe Ely's Christmas party in Austin one year and now the salad and I get an annual invite to attend the popular rock singer's party.

Whole chicken
Baking bag
½ cup celery, chopped
1 cup fried bacon, crumbled
½ cup sliced black olives
2 avocados
¼ tsp. salt
¼ tsp. pepper
½ tsp. garlic powder
½ cup pecans, toasted and chopped
Mayonnaise

Season whole chicken and cook in a baking bag until meat falls off the bone. Let cool, debone and cool meat in the ice box. Now toast the pecans on a cookie sheet or in the microwave until toasted but not too dark. (Pecans will be crunchy after they cool.) Dice the avocados. Chop cooled chicken meat the size of playing dice. Mix in the celery, bacon, olives, pecans and seasonings, then the avocados, stirring after each addition. Add mayonnaise to taste; I use about a cup.

PEARL'S TURKEY SALAD
Texas

You can please your family and save yourself a lot of cooking time in the kitchen by simply spicing up your holiday leftovers. My menfolk love this one.

Leftover turkey, medium-sized bowlful
2 T. onion, chopped
1 kid-size box of raisins
1 crisp red apple
½ cup sweet pickles, chopped

Cut leftover turkey into diced cubes. Mix all ingredients together. Serve on whole wheat bread.

PHOEBE'S CHICKEN CLIMAX
Texas

Phoebe Burkhalter and her husband Farley are little people. Walking into their house, with all their little furniture that Farley makes out in his woodshop, is like a bad carnival ride. The little TV set on a the little hand-made TV stand makes you feel like you're in "Alice In Wonderland". I couldn't sit in the little chairs they have, so Phoebe served me this dish out on the front porch where I felt less dizzy. She makes a little of it for Farley every Friday night. Here's the recipe in Pheobe's own words.

> 2 chicken breasts
> 1 egg
> 1 glop of milk
> ½ cup flour
> Cornflakes
> Olive oil
> 3 T. butter
> Cheap white wine
> 1 can cream of mushroom soup
> Salt and pepper
> Oregano
> Sweet basil
> Paper sack (for shaking up chicken)
> One stool (for seeing over the stove)

"Kill one chicken and rip out its breast. Beat one egg lightly with a glop of milk. Add salt and pepper to mixture and set aside.

"Wash off them breasts, throw 'em in a brown paper sack with ½ cup flour, and I throw in four handfuls of crushed up cornflakes. (That's probably one handful for big people.) Shake 'em up good in the sack, but close it first.

"Heat ¼ inch of olive oil in a medium skillet over a medium flame until a water drop thrown in sizzles right off. Take them breasts out of the sack, dip 'em in the egg mixture and drop 'em in the skillet. Brown both sides. Remove breasts from skillet, pour off the oil, wipe out the pan, turn burner down real low, add about 3 tablespoons of butter to skillet and put breasts back in. Pour some cheap white wine over them breasts, season with lots of oregano and sweet basil.

"Put a lid on the skillet then leave it simmering for 15 minutes or so while you read the funny papers. Spoon in 1 can of condensed cream of mushroom soup on top of them breasts, add some more oregano and basil, and replace the lid. Continue simmering over low heat for another 20 minutes. Eat them breasts with the mushroom gook in the pan spread over them and serve with Cheryl's rice."

BERTHA'S BEEF
Texas

Bertha Bumiller is an excellent cook but most of the time she's too busy with Tuna activities to do much fancy cooking. She does serve a special steak dish that her family loves and if you can ever get her away from a "Smut Snatcher" meeting long enough, she'll make it. I asked her to write this recipe down for me and after two months and several phone calls to remind her, the recipe is at last recorded for all to enjoy.

> **3 lbs. top round steak, 3-inches thick**
> **2 pieces of beef suet, 2-inches each**
> **1 T. butter**
> **3 large yellow onions, chopped (about 2 cups)**
> **1 T. salt**
> **Boiling water**

Cut the steak into 3-inch cubes. Heat suet and butter in a large, deep skillet or Dutch oven. Add chopped onions and cook until tender and browned. Remove from skillet and set aside.

Put meat into hot skillet and brown thoroughly on all sides. Be sure not to turn the meat until it starts to stick to the skillet. Return the onions to the skillet and sprinkle with salt. Add enough boiling water to almost cover the meat. Cover and bring to a boil; immediately lower the heat and simmer 1 hour, or until meat is very tender. Remove the meat to a hot platter. Make a gravy by thickening the pan liquid with a mixture of flour and water. Add seasoning if needed. Pour gravy over meat. Makes 10–12 servings.

SMAXIE'S SPAGHETTI SAUCE
Texas

Smaxie is from Waxahachie, Texas, and now lives in Tuna. Her cooking is in big demand at Texas banquets that feed lots of people, so her name comes up a lot in catering circles. She married a man named Tony from Little Italy, New York. They met at a Holiday Inn banquet and he immediately put her in marriage and business making his mom's Italian sauce. The business to this day is served well by mama's recipe. Tony and Smaxie separated when Tony fell in love with an Apache woman who made the best fry bread Smaxie said she'd ever eaten. "Tony took my heart, but he left me that business and the recipe."

2 T. dried basil
1 T. oregano
3 sprigs parsley, chopped
1 T. salt
½ T. pepper
2 T. sugar
Olive oil
¼ cup red wine
1 large onion, chopped
1 clove garlic, chopped finely
2 celery stalks, chopped
½ lb. mushrooms or 2 cups, sliced
1 28-oz. can Progresso Tomato Puree
1 10-oz. can whole peeled tomatoes
1 cup Pomi strained tomatoes
1 small can tomato paste

In 3 tablespoons of olive oil, saute until transparent the chopped onion and celery. Add garlic and cook until you can smell it. Do not brown garlic. Reduce to a simmer or warm.

In a 4 quart pan heat the tomato puree and the whole peeled tomatoes. Mix together well and chop the tomato a bit. Add sauted mixture to this and now add the Pomi tomatoes and the chopped parsley. Mix well. In a separate skillet, heat 1 tablespoon olive oil and then add 3 tablespoons of tomato paste (or ½ small can), stir constantly, cooking the paste until it darkens and is scorched well but not burned. Add this to the sauce, mixing in well. Add wine after this and now the mushrooms.

Reduce to a simmer and cook 2 hours or more, stirring every now and then. If too thick, add more Pomi tomatoes and adjust seasoning to taste. This sauce is excellent for all meatball dishes and especially lasagna.

BOSTON MEAT BALLS
Massachusetts

All mothers have a spaghetti recipe because kids love it, but lots of folks never take the time to do meatballs properly. Surprise your family with these on Wednesday night, and if you know of someone who's getting married, this is a sure recipe to give her.

    1 lb. lean ground beef
    1 lb. ground sausage
    1 bell pepper, chopped fine
    1 onion, finely chopped
    1 T. garlic powder
    ½ tsp. salt
    ½ tsp. pepper
    1 egg

Mix beef, sausage, bell pepper, onion, egg and seasoning by hand. Roll into semi-tight balls, the size of a golf ball. Brown the balls of meat in a skillet until done. Drain and add to Smaxies's Spaghetti Sauce or any commercial brand.

JUNE'S CLASSIC HAMBURGER
Oklahoma

Everyone makes good hamburgers but June makes her's the diner way. Most restaurant hot grills cook lots of various foods on top of each other's juices. June places a few cut up onions and one strip of bacon in the bottom of her hamburger skillet. Patties cook out on this bed of tastes which are not necessarily added to the final sandwich. This and other secrets below create that diner hamburger taste at home.

> Hamburger patties flattened to 1-inch thick
> 1 small onion, chopped
> 1 or 2 strips of bacon
> Salt and pepper to taste
> American or cheddar cheese
> Hamburger buns

Cook patties on a scattered bed of chopped onion and strip(s) of bacon. Add cheese to the top when desired amount of cooking is reached. Place bottom bun on top of cheese and top bun goes on top of the bottom bun. Cover and simmer 4 minutes or until cheese is melted. Drain off excess fat before cheese and buns go on. Do not let the grease soak up in the buns.

HOT HAMBURGERS
Little America Truckstop
U.S.A.

All hard working men like truck stop food. It's fun to make every now and then just to see their faces light up. My nephew loves this recipe and I'll make it for him only if he peels the potatoes.

Hamburger patty
French fries
Toast
Beef gravy (any recipe or canned)

This dish is laid out with two pieces of toast, one piece whole, one piece sliced on the diagonal. These are placed on the bottom of an oval plate or large dish. On top of this place a hamburger pattie that has been flattened out, just like they cook 'em in a diner. Over this put your fresh cut, French fried potatoes and pour on the hot beef gravy.

PEARL'S STOVE-TOP FAJITAS
Texas

Fajitas are a favorite among native Texans. My old friend James Gonzales says his grandmother cooked them in the fields of South Texas. According to James this "skirt steak", as it's called today, was a throw away section when wealthy ranchers butchered cattle. This throw away was given to the Mexican cooks and they beat the meat into tenderness using spices as they pounded. You can bet there were plenty of these fajitas around the King Ranch where they operated one of Texas' largest slaughter houses. I learned this stove-top technique from Jaston Williams but the ingredients here are my own. My recipe is far from true Mexican, but James loves these and I'm always surprised by how many he can eat. Serve with Rodriquez Guacamole.

2 to 3 lbs. sliced skirt steak (tenderized)
1 regular sized bottle of Kraft Italian Dressing
2 tsp. Fajita seasoning
1 large onion, chopped
1 large tomato, chopped
Grated cheese
Shredded lettuce
Flour tortillas (fresh package)

Slice skirt steak into strips 3 inches long and 1 inch in width. Season meat with fajita seasoning. Place meat in a bowl and cover with entire bottle of Italian dressing. Marinate at least 2 hours, preferably overnight. Turn all the meat and marinade into a skillet and begin cooking at medium heat. Add onions and stir slightly. You can raise the heat but don't cook too fast. Be careful to not let them stick, so stir often until most of the oil and marinade is cooked-up and the meat is more than well-done. (Traditional fajitas are not rare or even medium-well, but overcooked.) Drain meat on paper towels. Warm up tortillas on flat pan or skillet at medium to low heat. Turn tortillas until both sides are hot. Place fajita meat in a tortilla and add condiments of choice: tomatoes, lettuce, cheese and/or guacamole.

RODRIQUEZ GUACAMOLE SALAD
Texas

Cindy Rodriquez lives in San Antonio, Texas. To get this recipe out of her, I had to invite the talkative woman over to my house several times so she could make it. She follows no rules or order but does plenty of talking as she makes it; rarely looking into the bowl other than to not miss it when she adds ingredients.

> 4 or 5 ripe avocados
> 2 T. sour cream
> Garlic powder, to taste
> 1 small onion, finely chopped
> 1 medium tomato, chopped
> 3 sprigs fresh, chopped parsley
> 1 tsp. salt, or less to your taste
> ¼ tsp. pepper
> 1 T. lemon juice

Mash avocado and sour cream with a potato masher. Add garlic powder to taste (don't be afraid to use more). Add onion, tomato and salt while mixing and mashing. Now stir in parsley, pepper and lemon juice. Try to serve fresh, as cooling can cause avocados to turn brown.

LAS MANITAS FAJITAS
Austin, Texas

Las Manitas Cafe in downtown Austin, Texas, is without a doubt Austin's most popular Mexican food. This wait-in-line restaurant is owned and operated by a couple of feisty sisters named Cynthia and Libby. I've been eating these fajitas since they opened their doors in the early 1980s. It's the first place I stop when Henry and I visit Governor Richards in Austin. Cynthia is a hard working woman noted for her no-nonsense approach to good business and we're honored to have the cafe's noted recipe. It's not given out to just anybody.

> 4 lbs. fajita meat
> 1 to 2 onions, chopped
> 2 to 3 cloves fresh garlic
> Black pepper to taste
> 1½ cup fresh squeezed lime juice, enough to cover meat

Marinate the fajita meat in above ingredients for one day. When you're ready to cook, start a fire in the barbeque pit.

When you're ready to cook, start a fire in the barbeque pit. Las Manitas Avenue Cafe uses mesquite wood because it tastes best and wood burns cleaner than charcoal. The smoke from the mesquite sears the meat and allows all the juices to remain inside. The meat must be handled gently with tongs, never a knife or fork, so as not to puncture the meat. Throw all the onions and the extra marinating ingredients on the fire to season the smoke. Cook for 15 to 30 minutes depending on the intensity of the fire. Fajitas are ready to eat when the meat "sponges up". To be perfectly sure it's done, cut into one piece to see if it's cooked completely. Wrap meat in a tortilla and serve with the traditional fajita garnishments. Serves six to eight people.

VENISON LOAF
Texas

Having family living out in the Texas Hill Country, I know how many of you love deer meat. I could never stand it myself, but my husband loved it and I prepared it anyway. I got myself a good old Southern recipe for venison and Henry has always loved it. It's a sure cure for those husbands wanting to be hunters and in Texas there are plenty of white tail deer to accommodate. This is an old Southern recipe that works for me.

> 1 lb. ground venison
> ½ lb. ground pork sausage
> 1 egg
> ½ cup dried bread crumbs
> 1 cup milk
> 1½ tsp. salt
> ½ T. minced onion

Mix the meats together, then add the egg, milk, bread crumbs and seasoning. Put it all in a greased pan and bake it for 1 hour in a 350° oven. This serves four.

COWBOY STEW
Wyoming

These cowboys are exposed to some fine cooking out West but often find themselves out on a "drive" without one of those chefs of the prairie. So this dish is made from a commercial seasoning mix (Beef Stew). All other ingredients should be fresh. After your hired hands eat this stew you might get them to help dress those eight pullets you need for Sunday's Social.

3 quarts of water
1 ½ lbs. of stew meat
Beef stew mix or packet (commercial brand)
1 large onion, chopped
1 ear of corn or 1 can of whole kernel corn
2 large russet potatoes, cubed small
1 package of fresh frozen peas (or 1 can peas)
3 medium carrots, sliced
Salt and pepper to taste

Season meat with salt and pepper. Place meat in 3 quarts of water along with chopped onion. Bring to a boil. Add water if too much boils away. Add seasoning from commercial mix when meat becomes well done or semi-tender. Stir well.

Cook another 15 minutes at a lower heat. Add the carrots, potatoes, peas, and corn. (Cut kernels off ear before cooking.) Stir well and cover. Simmer over low heat for another hour, stirring as often as you can. Stew will thicken more than soup. When your meat falls apart to the touch, your Cowboy Stew is ready. Serve with the cowboy favorite - saltine crackers.

PEARL AND VERA'S QUICHE
Texas

Our Baptist preacher, 'Reverend Spikes' first wife, Mimi, was French Canadian and the most persnickety woman you'll ever meet. Living with Spikes must have been hell enough but Mimi hated everything about Tuna, Texas. She didn't like the town, the people, the weather and especially the traditional Baptist meals Norma Wooten served after the Sunday service. So one Sunday, Vera Carp and I made this quiche for Mimi who never stopped bragging about it. Later she and Spikes separated; rumor has it that Mimi had insisted on wine with her Baptist meals. As she left town for good, she was quoted by the attendant at Bernie Berkhalter's service station as saying, "This town isn't worth the tumbleweeds it's built on, except for Pearl and Vera's Quiche." Vera always said Mimi needed to find a good Catholic family where she'd fit in.

½ cup bacon, cooked and diced
1 cup ground sausage, cooked
1 cup chopped onion
½ cup diced mushrooms
½ cup chopped broccoli, uncooked
2 cups shredded Swiss or American cheese
1 unbaked pastry shell, 10-inch
2 eggs, slightly beaten
1 cup milk
½ tsp. salt
⅛ tsp. pepper
1½ T. garlic powder

Fry the bacon and keep half the grease. Add onion, mushrooms and garlic powder and cook until onion is soft. Turn contents of skillet into a mixing bowl. Add crumbled bacon and sprinkle with cheese. Add the cooked ground sausage and the broccoli, stirring well. Pour a mixture of eggs, milk, pepper and salt over this and stir again. Turn entire mixture into the pastry shell. Bake at 375° for 35 to 45 minutes or until lightly browned. Serve hot or warm. Add fresh fruit as a side dish.

DIDI'S TUNA FRANKS
New York

Didi Snavely does not live in New York but she loved this prize winning recipe. Didi runs the used weapons store in Tuna, Texas, and she hates the microwave oven. It was with this recipe that she almost exploded her microwave when she placed these tin-foil-wrapped Tuna Franks in it. "Nobody told me a goddamn thing about those ovens when I bought it." Didi now uses a conventional oven as the recipe requires.

    1 large can tuna fish
    ½ cup chopped onion
    ½ cup chopped celery
    ½ cup black olives
    ½ cup chopped hard boiled egg
    ½ cup chopped sweet pickles
    1 cup grated American cheese
    1 cup mayonnaise (at least)
    Hot dog buns
    Tin foil for wrapping buns

Mix first eight ingredients together adding more mayonnaise if necessary. Fill a hot dog bun with the mixture, wrap buns individually and rather loosely in tin foil and bake at 400° for 10 minutes or until cheese is melted inside buns.

JAMES' TROUT
Wyoming - Texas

James catches trout in Yellowstone National Park and serves them immediately. He prefers fried trout, fried red snapper and bass all prepared the same way. He catches them himself so I guess he can eat them any way he chooses. If you're a fried fish eater like James, you'll never go wrong with his process for cooking it.

Fillets of trout, red snapper, or bass cut in
  2-inch squares
2 cups cornmeal
½ cup flour
Salt and pepper to taste
Crisco shortening

In a frying pan, heat Crisco on medium-high. Soak fish fillets in water. Drain and lightly season with salt and pepper. Mix cornmeal and flour in a bowl. Roll fish lightly in cornmeal mixture then put in the hot frying pan. Make sure there's enough grease so pieces can float. Do not cover. Turn fish over when pieces turn golden brown. Drain on paper towels and serve with salad and fried potatoes.

JEAN'S BEEF & CABBAGE CASSEROLE
Oklahoma

I love to eat at Jean's house. You can depend on her cooking to take you back to days when the taste of food caused you to say "somebody's been cooking all day." Seconds are in big demand around her lunch table, but don't stay around too long. Once her soap operas begin, she's no good to anybody.

1 medium head cabbage, shredded
1 lb. hamburger meat
1 onion, chopped
½ cup rice, uncooked
1 can Campbell's Tomato Soup
Water
Pinch of saffron powder

Place shredded cabbage in a greased baking dish. Brown hamburger meat with the chopped onion. Stir in ½ cup uncooked rice. Place meat/onion/rice mixture in a nest made in the center of the cabbage. Cover with tomato soup and 1 can of water. Add a pinch of saffron powder. Cover and bake in a 350° oven for about 1 hour.

BARBARA STANWYCK STEAK
Hollywood

My husband Henry was a great fan of this steak and movie actress. Barbara's favorite way of eating steak was simple, yet quite sophisticated in flavor. I've had this recipe for years and don't remember where I got it, but I preserved it for future generations. Serve on TV trays as you watch "American Movie Classics".

½ cup soy sauce
1 tsp. brown sugar
¼ tsp. black pepper
1 tsp. olive oil
1 club steak or small porterhouse steak
2 T. butter

Mix soy sauce with the brown sugar, pepper and olive oil. Pour into a shallow pan. Put steak into this sauce and spoon a little sauce over the top. Marinate for 30 minutes, turning several times. Heat a large, heavy skillet. Cook the steak over high heat until charred on one side; turn and cook quickly until charred on the other side. The result is steak charred on the outside, but pink in the middle. Serve on a well heated platter.

PAUL'S ADOBO
Philippine Islands

I met Paul in the "outback down under" when I had stepped in a Kangaroo pile. He was nice about explaining the origins of the pile and I was so fascinated with his interest in it that we had lunch together. He prepared "Adobo" and I've been making it ever since. I throw away the bones after the meat is tender. Paul leaves them in for flavor.

Paul: "It could be said that this is the national dish of the Philippine Islands. It was taught to me in 1982 on a visit to the Islands."

> 1 lb. of chicken
> 1 lb. of pork
> 1 T. vinegar
> 1½ T. soy sauce
> 1 bay leaf
> Black pepper to taste, optional

Cut meat into cubes and place in a large saucepan with all other ingredients. Cover and cook for ½ hour on low heat, stirring occasionally. Remove the meat and saute in a large saucepan or wok until meat is brown. Return meat to the original saucepan, cover and cook on low heat, stirring occasionally, for 1½ hours or until meat is tender. Serve with rice and salad. Serves four.

VEGETABLES & SIDE DISHES

Photo by Scott Newton

Rex is a reformed egg sucker, and the first graduate of
Pearl's recovering egg sucker program.

C.H.'S BISCUITS AND GRAVY
Kansas

C. H. is one of those old fools you can count on for something silly. I don't know a man on this earth who has more friends and he'll cook you up a batch of these biscuits any time you ask. I just let him go to it on this recipe, so hang in there and enjoy his sense of humor and the best breakfast you'll ever eat. His gravy is rare in that it always comes out just the right thickness. If you're worried that "what tastes good on the lips will go to the hips", back off on this one.

C. H. said, "Aunt Pearl, you can only use this biscuit recipe if you'll swear not to use the biscuits for your bitter pills. However, if you want to give folks a breakfast that not only fills stomachs, but puts smiles on faces, give 'er a go!

"First, make sure you're fully awake. There have been many a biscuit go down the tubes of the garbage disposal because the cook was too pie-eyed to negotiate the recipe. If it takes a pot of coffee to accomplish this, let your pot perk you into full alertness before proceeding further. Also, if you want to cheat, break out the Bisquick and follow the instructions on the box. But for the true challenge of "biscuitry", try the following list of ingredients."

2 cups flour
¼ tsp. cream of tartar
4 tsp. baking powder
½ tsp. salt
1 T. sugar (optional)
½ cup Crisco
⅔ cup milk

"Being a cigar smoker and knowing other cooks who smoke as well, I caution you to extinguish your smoke before mixing these ingredients. It's very difficult to disguise a cigar ash in your biscuits.

"Combine the dry ingredients and sift into a medium-sized mixing bowl. Using a pastry cutter or fork, cut the Crisco into the dry ingredients until the mixture is like coarse meal. Add the milk to mix the dough. Do not over mix.

"Put dough on floured board and knead a few times. Roll out your dough to a 1 inch thickness. Powder your dough with flour. To cut the biscuits, you can use a fancy biscuit cutter or, if you're like me, use a water glass for a king-sized biscuit or a juice glass for a tea-sized biscuit. Press cutter into flour before cutting the dough or you'll have dough on your drinking glasses for weeks to come. Pop the cut biscuits onto an ungreased cookie sheet. I like to give my biscuits breathing room, so leave appropriate space between them. However, others like their biscuits stuck together, so if you're one of these, allow biscuits to gently touch one another. Bake in a pre-heated oven at 450° for about 8 to 10 minutes. It's alright to peek at them occasionally. In higher altitudes bake at 475°.

"As the biscuits are baking, brown your sausage in a frying pan. If you accumulate a lot of grease, pour some of it off, otherwise you'll not need an oil change for six months. Now add 2 tablespoons of flour into the frying pan, mixing it with the sausage and grease. Pour 2 cups of milk into the pan and stir. Salt and pepper to taste. Stir frequently as you bring the gravy to a boil. This should eliminate those lumps so common with oatmeal and gravy. Do not overcook or your gravy will only be good for paving your driveway.

"Remove baked biscuits from the oven, break open and butter, add a generous portion of gravy (make 'em swim), and serve. Now you're ready to cut firewood, bale hay, churn the butter and walk 20 miles. Enjoy!"

PEARL'S BAKED BEANS
Texas-Oklahoma

I've been making this taste bud delight since the 1940s. In fact I was stirring in the final ingredient when President Roosevelt announced we were going after the Japanese for Pearl Harbor. Later I went to work in Houston for the war effort and shared this side dish with other "Rosie the Riveters".

2 cans Campbell's Pork & Beans
4 strips bacon
½ green bell pepper, chopped
1 small yellow onion, chopped
½ cup brown sugar
½ cup ketchup
1 T. mustard
1 T. sweet pickle juice
No salt or pepper

Use a deep or a long, shallow dish. Mix together all ingredients except bacon strips. Crumble brown sugar in as you stir. Place bacon strips across top of recipe. Bake at 350° until beans start to boil. Reduce heat to 325° and cook until bacon strips are done. Cook for about an hour, don't stir the beans after baking begins and don't let them get too dry. Remember the deep dish will take longer to cook than a shallow dish.

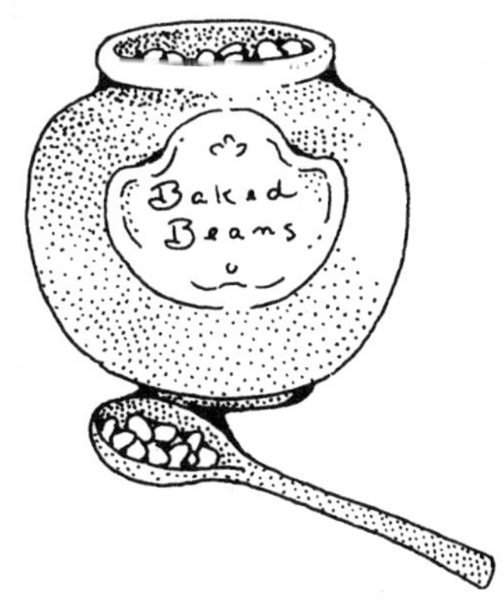

AUNT PEARL'S POTATO SALAD
Texas

I take this salad to large picnics and reunions where other covered dishes appear. It's so good, the other womenfolk quit bringing potato salad 'cause they know mine is the best!

5 pound bag of brown Idaho potatoes
1 dozen eggs
1½ cup chopped sweet pickles
Small can evaporated milk
1 cup celery, diced small
1 cup finely chopped yellow onion
2 cups or more of Miracle Whip or Mayonnaise
2 T. mustard
¼ cup sweet pickle juice
Salt and pepper

Boil potatoes in their skins until tender. Drain water and let potatoes cool down to room temperature. Peel off skins and let whole potatoes sit in ice box. (They cut better cold and don't crumble.)

Boil eggs, drain and let cool to room temperature. Separate white and yellow. Chop 2 cups of white and mash all the yolk with a fork. Mix the eggs with ¼ teaspoon black pepper and ½ teaspoon salt.

Mix evaporated milk with the eggs. Mix in ¼ cup of sweet pickle juice. Stir in celery, sweet pickles, and onions. Stir in mayonnaise and mustard. This mixture should now be a thick, cake-like batter texture and may need more mayo. Let this mixture cool and marinate in ice box for 1 hour.

Dice the cold potatoes into pieces the size of playing dice. Season potatoes with 1 teaspoon salt and ¼ teaspoon pepper. (Salt is very important in this recipe and if you don't have enough, the flavor of the salad is flat.) Pour mixture over potatoes and stir with large forks. Large utensils used to stir can sometimes inhibit getting all the potatoes covered with dressing. You may need to add more mayo to cover all pieces with a thick creamy coating. Serve with Pearl's Baked Beans for a compatible duo of tastes.

VIRGINIA'S BEAN SALAD
Arkansas

Virginia is a classic country cook. She supplies us here with her famous three bean salad recipe.

2 cans of Brown Beauty beans (or kidney)
1 medium onion
½ medium green bell pepper
1 large tomato
5 eggs, hard boiled
1 to 2 large dill pickles
¼ cup pickle juice
¾ cup mayonnaise
¼ cup mustard
¾ cups celery, including leafy tops
½ tsp. celery seed
½ tsp. celery salt
½ tsp. garlic powder
1 tsp. parsley flakes
Salt and pepper to taste

Drain beans. Dice all other vegetables and the eggs. Mix all together. In a separate bowl, mix mayonnaise and mustard with the pickle juice. Add this to the beans and stir in well. Add seasonings and mix all ingredients. Refrigerate overnight. Serve cool to a crowd. This recipe makes a bunch.

JUNE'S CORN ON THE COB
Oklahoma

Southerners love and demand corn-on-the-cob but be mindful that this is an easy vegetable to overcook. For the perfect flavor and right amount of cooking, follow this one closely. It's simple.

A large pan of water with lid is required. Stir in 1 teaspoon of salt to water. Bring to a hard boil. Place corn in boiling water and cover. (Do not add corn to unboiled water.) Cover and cook at a boil for 10 minutes. Drain water, add butter and serve hot.

NEW ORLEANS CREOLE BEANS
Louisiana

This is it, the real thing. This recipe is an all-star find. I learned this classic dish from Cheryl Hawkins, a New Orleans native who could not cook anything else if her life depended on it. Her grandmother, Mimi, a French woman, could not cook any more and made young Cheryl follow her explicit directions. (Cheryl's hands doing what her grandmother's could not.) Cheryl made this family recipe so many times that she never forgot it. Her grandmother's Creole Beans are classic in taste. You must pay attention to her grandmother's instructions, just as Cheryl did. Serve over rice.

> 1 lb. dried Red Beans or Kidney Beans
> 2 smoked hamhocks
> 1 lb. sliced smoked sausage
> 1 large red onion, chopped fine
> 1 bunch green onions, chopped fine
> 1 large bell pepper, chopped fine
> 2 cloves fresh garlic, chopped fine
> 2 sticks butter, not margarine

Soak beans overnight in water. In a large bean pot, cover beans with four inches of fresh water. Add hamhocks and sausage and bring to a boil for 1 hour.

Saute red onions, bell pepper, green onions and garlic in one stick of butter. After garlic starts to brown, turn heat off and let sit. Add sauted vegetables to boiled beans. Stir well and reduce heat to medium and cook at a low boil for 30 minutes. Add another stick of butter to beans and stir until melted. Cover beans and reduce heat to low and cook until mixture turns a thick stew-like substance or until hamhocks fall apart and the beans can be smashed easily with a fork. (About 1½ hours). Stir beans frequently and always add boiling water when more water is needed. Serve over Cheryl's Rice.

Cheryl's Rice

2 cups rice
½ tsp. salt
1 tsp. oil

Cover rice with one inch of water. Stir in salt and oil. Bring to a hard boil while stirring. Reduce heat to simmer, cover and cook 25 minutes.

BIDDY'S NOODLES
Oklahoma

This is the most sought after recipe in this book. Biddy's noodles have them standing on their heads for more. The New York Post printed this old noodle recipe because of its historical preparation out on the prairies and yet this same process is still used today. I cook these every holiday with turkey as does June and Jean who also learned this recipe from Biddy. The knack is drying the noodles before cooking. I leave mine rolled out on a table with floured waxed paper for at least four hours. June lets her's dry about an hour and Jean claims she tried drying her noodles on the clothesline once and the birds ate them. Jean provides the written process below and recommends you follow her instructions on drying the noodles.

    4 eggs
Half and half cream
¼ tsp. baking powder
Flour
Salt

Beat eggs slightly and add 4 measurements of half and half. (A measurement is made here in half of an egg shell.) Add ½ tsp. salt and a pinch (¼ tsp.) of baking powder. Add enough flour to thicken mixture enough to roll on a floured board to ¼ inch thickness. Let stand until almost dry and cut into strips. Add noodles slowly to hot boiling turkey broth and a few at a time. Cook until done to taste - about 12 minutes covered and 12 minutes uncovered. Stir often as they burn easily. Noodle gravy and noodles are served over stuffing.

OLD LADY CABBAGE
Georgia

I discovered this dish in Atlanta. It's a favorite recipe for old folks and appears a lot at senior campouts and among RV-trailer travel groups. Cabbage is a health food and is not considered a favorite among a lot of men. It takes an old cook with many year's experience to come up with a good cabbage dish that men will like.

> 1 head of cabbage
> 2 lbs. hamburger meat, very lean (This dish is not drained so you need to use lean meat. Regular ground will have too much fat.)
> 2 large onions, chopped
> 1 large can of tomato sauce
> Salt and pepper
> Garlic powder

Use a large, stove top pot as this recipe needs room and height. First, place a layer of onion on bottom of pan. Follow with a layer of meat. Season lightly with salt, pepper and garlic powder. Add a layer of cabbage, then a layer of tomato sauce over the cabbage. Spread with fingers.

Repeat layers starting with the onion on top of meat. You may have two, three or even four layers, but keep the layers in order. And remember, don't stir the layers. Cover and cook on top of the stove over low heat. Cooking time can be an hour or more depending on how mushy you like your cabbage. I overcook this dish to the point that the cabbage starts to turn brownish. Remove lid when cabbage and meat are well done. Let sit on stove until serving.

DOLLY MAY'S SCALLOPED POTATOES
Oklahoma

Dolly May's husband baled hay for a living and Dolly found herself baking for lots of field hands and hay workers. Men love this dish year round but oven heat keeps me making it only in winters. This is a newlywed recipe, so get used to making it regularly like I have.

**4 or 5 large potatoes
2 large onions
½ cup milk
4 T. butter
Salt and pepper**

Into a baking dish put a layer of thinly sliced potatoes, salt, pepper and pats of butter. Then add a layer of onions with dots of butter, salt and pepper. Repeat until all potatoes and onions are used. Pour milk over potatoes and onions to cover them. Use more milk if needed. Cook in a moderate oven until potatoes are well browned. Serves six.

SOPHIE'S BROCCOLI SOUP
Texas

Sophie is the upstanding President of the "Ladies For a Better Tuna". Her organization puts on the big 4th of July celebration each year here in Tuna Town Park. Nobody misses her club meetings because Sophie always serves this soup.

6 T. chopped onion
2 T. oil
2 cans chicken broth
4 ounces fine noodles
1 pkg. chopped frozen broccoli
3 cups milk
8 ounces American grated cheese
Salt and pepper

Bring onions, oil, and chicken broth to a boil. Now add noodles. Cook 3 or 4 minutes. Add the package of chopped, frozen broccoli. When it is heated, add the milk and cheese and stir until the cheese is melted. Salt and pepper to taste.

COPPER PENNIES
Louisiana

This is the best carrot dish I've ever eaten. My cajun friend, Beth, said she got this recipe from her friend Kathy and now the world has it. If broccoli were carrots, George Bush would love this dish.

1 lb. package of carrots, peeled and sliced
½ bunch of green onion, sliced
¼ cup apple cider vinegar
¼ cup of water, reserved from boiling
½ cup sugar, or to taste (Beth's family likes it sweet.)

Bring carrots to a good boil, cover and set aside to cool. Carrots should be kind of crisp and not too soft. Drain carrots. When cool, mix onions with enough cider vinegar, water, and sugar to cover carrots. Refrigerate overnight. Serve cool.

BREADS
&
SWEETS

Photo by Scott Newton

ENID'S ORANGE BRAN MUFFINS
Texas

People who have seen me in "A Tuna Christmas" have asked about Enid's Orange Bran Muffins. She wins ribbons for them about as often as Vera Carp wins the Christmas Yard Display competition. She's one of my best customers and she tells everyone that she uses my eggs. It's Opal's influence on the other hens, I know it is.

½ cup whole bran cereal
½ cup orange juice
1 ¾ cups sifted, all purpose flour
2 tsp. baking powder
¼ tsp. baking soda
½ teaspoon salt
¼ cup honey
½ cup shortening
1 egg
¼ cup milk
½ cup drained, crushed pineapple

Mix bran and orange juice together and set aside. In another bowl sift together flour, baking powder, baking soda and salt. In a large bowl cream sugar and shortening. Then add one egg and beat until light and fluffy. Add the dry ingredients alternately with the milk and the bran/orange juice mixture. Do not overmix. Add crushed pineapple. Spoon mixture into greased tins and bake at 400° for 20 minutes.

NORMA'S CORNBREAD
Texas

Norma Wooten is my neighbor here in Tuna, Texas. She's a nice woman who never causes me trouble. She lives with her unmarried daughter, Nadine, and they lead a quiet life. Norma used to be neurotic in the kitchen as she would always prepare huge portions of cornbread. She had cornbread soup, cornbread cookies, cornbread candy and if you want to see Nadine's odd-ball "tick" show up on her face, just mention cornbread out loud around her. Norma's doctor said it was time she slowed down and displayed some restraint on cooking cornbread. "Forget about Nadine not being married, you're not ever going to have grandchildren," he told her.

    ¼ **cup oil**
    1½ **cups yellow cornmeal**
    ½ **cup flour**
    3 **tsp. baking powder**
    2 **tsp. sugar**
    1 **egg**
    Milk

Heat the oven to 425°. Grease pan or tins. Put oil in pan, making sure the pan is well covered with a thin coat. Place the pan in a hot oven and heat.

In a bowl add milk and egg to the other ingredients (enough milk to make a fairly thick batter). Stir only enough to blend all the mix. Add hot oil from pan in oven, stir it in, then fill the hot baking pan with batter, making sure pan is not more than one third full. Bake for about 20–25 minutes or until brown.

NORMA'S CORNBREAD STUFFING
Texas

Norma bakes herself silly. She and her daughter live together in Tuna, but Norma makes big portions as if she was getting her daughter, Nadine, ready for marriage and a big group of kids. Reverend Spikes hired Norma to be the Sunday cook at Fellowship Hall in hopes she'd put her talent for large meals to work. Norma makes this cornbread stuffing twice a month down at the church and it's the only time I ever make it to the Sunday services. I use Norma's recipe for my Holiday Turkey stuffing. I use two "Opal eggs".

2 cups cornmeal
1 cup flour
3 tsp. shortening
1 tsp. salt
1 tsp. baking powder
1 cup milk
2 eggs
1 T. butter
1 cup chopped celery
1 cup chopped onion
2 slices toast, crumbled
Salt and pepper to taste
1 T. ground sage
About 2 cups turkey broth

Mix corn meal, flour, shortening, salt, baking powder, milk and eggs. Bake at 350° for about 45 minutes or until brown.

Crumble bread when cold. Saute onions and celery in the butter until transparent. Add this to cornbread, then crumble in the toast, add seasonings and moisten with the broth to desired consistency.

Return this to the oven for 30 minutes at 350°. You may want to pour another ¼ cup of broth over the top before the last baking if your mixture is too thick.

MISSY'S OATMEAL BREAD
Texas

Missy "Eagle Woman" Tatum is a diversified cook indeed. Her husband is a vegetarian, but she and the baby eat meat. When she sends her husband out to graze, she's cookin' up some fine meat loaf at home. Her bread is her husband's favorite and he likes it served with lots of steamed vegetables. I like the bread with meat loaf.

> 3 cups rolled oats
> 3 cups boiling water
> ½ cup toasted wheat germ
> 1 T. salt
> 2 T. oil
> ¼ cup honey
> 1 T. active dry yeast
> ½ cup warm water
> 5 to 5½ cups whole wheat flour
> ⅔ cup powdered milk

Put the rolled oats, oil, honey, salt, and toasted wheat germ in a large bowl. Pour boiling water over this mixture and let it cool to lukewarm. Dissolve yeast in ½ cup warm water. Add to the lukewarm rolled oats mixture. Sift the powdered milk with the flour and add it cup by cup to the liquid mixture. Knead thoroughly. When the dough begins to get stiff, turn it out onto a floured surface and work in the remaining milk and flour mixture.

Put the dough in a greased bowl and let it rise until it doubles in bulk. Punch it down, form it into two loaves, and place them seam-side down in two greased loaf pans. Let the loaves rise again until doubled in bulk. Preheat the oven to 400° as the loaves are rising. Bake for 45 minutes. This makes 2 loaves.

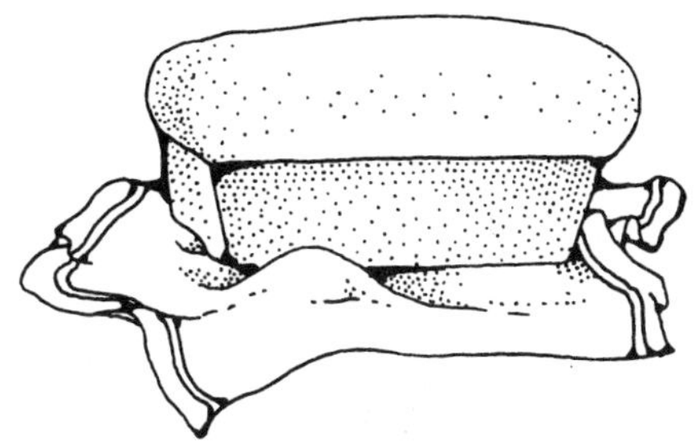

SOPHIE'S BROWN BREAD
South Dakota

Sophie enters this one each year at the Coweta County Fair and she's got the ribbons to prove it's good.

    2 cups boiling water
    2 T. margarine
    ¼ to ½ cup sugar
    14 T. Brer Rabbit (green label) molasses
    2 tsp. salt

Combine and cool to lukewarm. Then add:
    2 packages yeast dissolved in 1/3 cup lukewarm water

Add dark flour:
    2 to 2 ½ cups whole wheat or rye graham flour

Add about:
    4 cups white flour

Knead until dough holds together. Place dough in greased bowl and let rise until it doubles in bulk. Mold dough into loaf pans and let rise again. Bake at 425° for 15 minutes, then at 300° to 325° for about 30 minutes.

JUNE'S PIE CRUST
Oklahoma

Trust me, the secret is the ice water. Dolly May used this crust for her cobbler. Biddy taught her how to do it, as well as June and Jean. I don't know how it ended up being called June's Pie Crust, but there you have it. Those who master this pie crust will be the talk of the ladies at any gathering where men eat all the pie crust on their plate.

2 cups flour
1 cup Crisco
½ cup ice water
Pinch of salt

Blend flour and Crisco evenly, adding a pinch of salt. Use a pastry blender until particles are the size of small peas. Add ice water, mix well. Roll into two balls of dough and roll out on a floured surface into the shape of a large circle and shape this into the pie dish. Bake at 425° for 9–12 minutes or until light golden brown. Makes two 9-inch crusts or one double.

PEARL'S APPLE PIE
Texas

This is the only pie I make on a regular basis. I take it to celebrity parties and benefits with lovely pie crust flowers and leaf decorations on top. You can skip the decorations. It's classic in taste even without the fancy designs. After eating a slice of this pie my Henry always snuggles a little closer.

Pastry for 2-crust pie (see June's Pie Crust)
6-8 tart cooking apples
1 tsp. lemon juice
1 cup sugar
3 to 3½ tsps. flour
1 tsp. ground cinnamon
¼ tsp. nutmeg
⅛ tsp. salt
2 T. butter or margarine

Roll out 9-inch pie crust shell. Use remaining dough for top crust. Set aside. Wash, peel, quarter, core and thinly slice the apples. Slightly saute apples in 1 tablespoon of butter or margarine over medium heat. Remove from heat and pour mixture into a bowl. Drizzle with lemon juice. Toss lightly with mixture of sugar, flour, cinnamon, nutmeg and salt. (You can add a dash of allspice here if you like.)

Pour coated apples into the unbaked pie shell. Spread apples out evenly in pie shell. Dot apples with pats of butter. Add top crust and seal the seams where the pie crusts meet. Add five knife slits in top of pie. (Be decorative.) Bake at 450° for 10 minutes. Reduce heat to 350° and bake another 40 minutes or until pie crust turns a light brown.

Decorations

Roll remaining pie crust out thin and cut in the shape of flowers or leaves. Make sure most decorations touch the sides, you don't want too much weight in the center. Using a small artist's brush, apply half and half on the pie crust area to which you want to apply a decoration. Now brush top of decoration lightly. These coated decorations will bake darker than the other pie crust, so don't confuse decorations with the regular crust when looking for doneness.

MAXIE BOVINE'S PECAN PIE
Texas

Maxie is the only local Tuna gal to make it to the Miss Texas Pageant. Her cooking talents got her to the finals in Fort Worth and here's the pie that did it.

Maxie: "There are many varieties of pecan pie, but I believe the beauty of pecan pie is in its simplicity. Start with the best pecans and let their natural flavor come through. Just like every beauty contest I enter, I try to let my natural beauty come through. And even though I haven't won since 'Miss Tuna 1972', this pie is still a winner! Serve with coffee or my famous punch."

1 9-inch pie shell, unbaked
1 cup light corn syrup
½ cup sugar
¼ cup butter, melted
¼ tsp. salt
3 eggs, slightly beaten
1 tsp. vanilla or 1 T. bourbon
1 cup pecan pieces

In a saucepan combine corn syrup, sugar and butter and bring to a boil. Cool slightly and add salt and vanilla (or bourbon). Stirring constantly, mix slowly with eggs. Stir in pecans. Pour into unbaked pie shell and bake in preheated 350° oven on center rack for 40–50 minutes.

BOBBY'S SWEET POTATO PIE
Louisiana

Bobby Bridger makes this pie with whole foods and farm fresh eggs. In fact he used "Opal's eggs" for this recipe, but I was there when he broke the shells, just in case. This pie would be good in June's Pie Crust but to get this winning recipe right, you better follow what Bobby suggests.

Bobby: "Sweet potato pie is a staple of Louisiana as the state is famous for its yams. I learned this recipe from my Mother who I'm sure got it from her Mother and so forth. When I first moved to Texas 21 years ago, one of the things I missed most from Louisiana was the pie. Once I learned this recipe, I raised money to record *Heal In The Wisdom* by baking sweet potato pies for potential investors."

Whole Wheat Pie Crust

1½ cups of whole wheat flour
½ to ¾ tsp. salt
½ cup butter, well chilled
⅓ cup ice water

Sift the flour and salt together. Rapidly slice the cold butter and drop the slices into the flour. Use a sharp knife and cut the butter and flour until the mixture resembles coarse corn meal. Sprinkle the ice water over the mixture while kneading it with your bare hands until the dough gathers together. Form the dough into a ball, wrap it in wax paper and chill it for about two hours. When the dough is chilled, roll it out round and place it in the pie pan.

Pie Filling

Boil 3 medium-size sweet potatoes until well done. Flesh the potatoes out of their skins and put in a blender. Add three eggs, ½ cup of half and half, ½ stick of butter, one cup of maple syrup (Grade C is my favorite), and blend to a creamy consistency. Pour ingredients into the pie shell and bake at 350° until firm. Serve with whipped cream on top!

JEAN'S CUSTARD PIE
Oklahoma

Custard pie is a favorite among Grandpas and older men. Young people today love this in little pie crust tortes. It's an old American taste dating back to the Civil War and nobody has perfected this taste better than Jean. Her pies are served daily in Ruby Darby's restaurant.

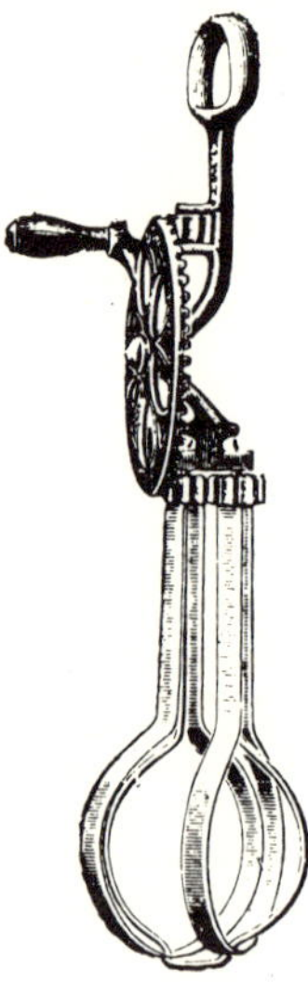

1 9-inch pie shell, unbaked
3 eggs
¾ cup sugar
¼ tsp. salt
¼ tsp. nutmeg
1 tsp. vanilla
2 ½ cups scalded milk

Beat eggs slightly. Add sugar and vanilla. Add scalded milk and nutmeg. Pour into the pie shell. Bake at 400° for 30 minutes or until knife inserted in center comes out clean.

VERA'S PEAR PIE
Texas

I have never liked this banker's wife, but when she brings this pie out for a gathering, the line always forms behind me. And since I'm first in line, Vera Carp always notices me and says, "Now Pearl, don't you eat all that pie by yourself, there are others."

¼ cup milk
1 cup brown sugar
6 pears
2 ready made pie crusts
¼ cup sliced almonds
1 stick butter
Ground cloves
Nutmeg
Cinnamon
1 small container sour cream
1 cup flour
1 maid
1 TV set
Comfortable shoes

Vera says, "Have your maid core and slice the pears. Make sure the knife she uses is not too sharp in case she decides to turn on you. One can never be too careful with minorities.

"Have your maid melt the butter in a medium size pot and add the pears. Add nutmeg, cloves and cinnamon to taste. That's your taste, not the maid's. Watch your favorite soap opera while maid simmers the pears. It may be helpful to look up the Spanish word for simmer.

"During commercials have your maid pour the simmered pears into a large pie crust. Have her cover the mixture with sliced almonds and over the entire mixture put sour cream. Use the other ready-made pie crust as a top crust. Have maid make small cuts in the top crust just like Betty Crocker would do. Pour milk over top crust to keep it moist and have maid place it in a pre-heated 400° oven for 10 minutes.

"Go back to watch soap operas while the maid cleans up the messy kitchen. Come back during the commercial and turn down the oven temperature to 350°. Have maid sit in front of oven window and watch pie cook for 25 to 30 minutes. Top crust will be light brown when the pie is cooked. Have maid remove the pie to cool while you count the silver. Drive maid home, or have her walk if the weather permits, then throw some flour around the kitchen so those pie crusts will appear to be homemade."

BIDDY'S IMPOSSIBLE PIE
Oklahoma

Biddy's store customers always looked forward to her "Impossible Pie". Biddy claims a lot of her recipes are from ladies magazines and the Family Weekly in the newspaper, but she can take a Betty Crocker recipe and make Sara Lee want to steal it. Her "Impossible Pie" is a yearly event and after you serve this to your group once, you'll be in the same boat each year too.

> ½ **cup sugar**
> ½ **cup Bisquick**
> **4 eggs**
> **2 cups milk**
> **1 tsp. vanilla**
> ½ **cup coconut**
> ½ **tsp. nutmeg**
> **4 T. margarine**

Mix all ingredients in a blender and pour into a pie pan. Cook 35 minutes in a 400° oven. It makes its own crust while baking.

AUNT ROSA'S
CHOCOLATE POUND CAKE
Texas

Iwanna and Inita Goodwin provided this delicious cake recipe. These are the wildest women I know and they drive over to my house and get "Opal eggs" to prepare this recipe. (I break open and inspect the eggs before they leave the house.) Inita cooks for the Tuna Tastee Kreeme and Iwanna sews for Penny's alteration department. Both of these hefty gals party hard and they like their men full of honky tonk fun. They sell Aunt Rosa's Chocolate Pound Cake each Christmas to pay for their annual "Domino's Pool Hall Party" on New Year's Eve. I always buy one of their cakes.

½ lb. margarine (2 sticks)
1 cup Crisco
3 cups sugar
5 Opal eggs
3 cups flour
½ tsp. salt
½ tsp. baking powder
5 T. cocoa
1 cup sweet milk
1 T. vanilla

Grease and flour the bottom of a 10-inch tube pan. In a mixing bowl, cream together butter, shortening and sugar. Add eggs one at a time, beating after each egg. Sift together flour, salt, baking powder and cocoa. Add this to the creamed mixture, alternately with the milk and vanilla, beating after each addition. Pour into the pan and bake at 325° for about 1½ hours. Cool in pan 5 minutes then turn out and cool more.

DOLLY'S PEACH COBBLER
Oklahoma

Dolly May was the "belle of the ball" and along with her sweet charm came one of our family's best country cooks. Her granddaughter, Charylene, has kept making this old-fashioned recipe just like Dolly. Charylene was reluctant to try the secret to Dolly's Peach Cobbler. It requires pouring a half cup of boiling water over the top before cooking. "I couldn't bring myself to pour a cup of water over this lively cobbler, but Grandma Dolly said to do it, so I closed my eyes and poured." Charylene prepares this for special family gatherings.

One pie crust for a deep dish pan
4 cups fresh peaches, sliced
1 cup sugar
3 tsp. flour
Butter
½ cup boiling water

Mix all ingredients except boiling water. Turn mixture into the pie crust and level, adding strips of left-over pie dough to make an informal lattice work on top. Place 'pats' of butter over top of crust. Pour boiling water over the top of all. Bake at 350° for about 50 minutes.

GRANNY'S RUM CAKE
Oklahoma

It's proper to have someone in the family record, execute and prepare perfectly the favorite recipe in the family. Kathy Vaughn is such an apprentice to her Granny's Rum Cake. Kathy is a child of the sixties who still remains dedicated to the ideals that her generation introduced to the world. Her concern over our planet and future generations of children remains steadfast and foremost in her life. As you make this fantastic rum cake, keep in mind Kathy's advice to children learning how to cook, "Whenever possible, cook with recycled products."

> 1 box yellow cake mix
> 1 small box vanilla pudding
> ½ cup rum
> ½ cup oil
> ½ cup water
> 4 eggs (I use "Opal eggs")
> 1 stick butter (½ cup)

Mix all together and bake at 325° for 55 to 60 minutes. Cool and glaze (recipe below).

Rum Glaze:

> 1 stick butter
> ½ cup rum
> ¼ cup sugar

Simmer over low to medium heat for a few minutes, stirring constantly. Pour over rum cake.

MARINA'S FESTIVE CRANBERRY TORTE
Texas

Marina had lost her famous recipe for 10 years and then a friend suggested she write the food editor of the San Antonio newspaper. She did and readers responded quickly with her favorite recipe. As Marina puts it, "So darlin', you know this is a good one." This is an ultimate taste experience for the holidays.

Crust:

1 ½ cups graham cracker crumbs
½ cup chopped pecans
¼ cup sugar
6 T. butter or margarine, melted

In a mixing bowl combine graham cracker crumbs, pecans, sugar, and the melted butter or margarine. Press onto bottom and up sides of an 8-inch springform pan. Chill.

Filling:

1½ cups ground fresh cranberries
   (start with 2 cups whole berries)
1 cup sugar
2 egg whites
1 T. frozen orange juice concentrate, thawed
1 tsp. vanilla
⅛ tsp. salt
1 cup whipping cream
Cranberry Glaze (recipe follows)
Fresh orange slices, quartered

In a large mixer bowl combine cranberries and 1 cup sugar; let stand 5 minutes. Add unbeaten egg whites, orange juice concentrate, vanilla, and salt. Beat on low speed of electric mixer till frothy. Then beat at high speed 6 to 8 minutes or till stiff peaks form (tips stand straight). In small mixer bowl whip the cream to soft peaks (tips curl over); fold into cranberry mixture. Turn into crust. Freeze firm.

To serve, remove torte from pan. Place on serving plate. Spoon Cranberry Glaze (see page 78) in center; place orange slices around outside. Makes 8 to 10 beautiful servings.

Cranberry Glaze

½ cup sugar
1 T. cornstarch
¾ cup fresh cranberries
⅔ cup water

In saucepan combine sugar and cornstarch, then stir in cranberries and water. Cook and stir till bubbly. Stir occasionally, just till cranberry skins pop. Cool to room temperature (do not chill). Makes 1 cup.

PEARL'S MOLASSES COOKIES
Texas-Oklahoma

This is one of my own. In a family of good cooks its nice to be recognized as the final word on old-fashioned cookies.

2½ cups flour
1 tsp baking powder
1½ tsp. ginger
1 tsp. salt
1 cup molasses
½ cup shortening (Crisco)
2 tsp. baking soda

Sift flour, baking powder, ginger and salt together. Heat molasses, remove from heat and add shortening and baking soda. Add flour mixture gradually to molasses. Chill dough for a couple of hours. Roll chilled dough very thin. Cut out cookies, place on greased cookie sheet and bake at 350° for 10 minutes. Remove from pan carefully, cool and store in a stone jar. Makes about 3 ½ dozen cookies.

GRANDMA COOKIES
Wyoming

Sue Fish lives in a beautiful valley south of Cody, Wyoming. She and her husband have a home between two pretty mountains, and their ranch is always filled with good cheer and these cookies. They're Aunt Pearl's favorites.

Sue: "Grandma always had a cookie can filled with these cookies as we grew up. She never used a recipe but a pinch of this and a handful of that. One Saturday I spent the day with Grandma, as this was her traditional baking day. By measuring her 'pinchfuls' and 'handfuls', the family got her recipe."

    ³/₄ cup butter or lard
    2 cups sugar
    ¹/₂ tsp. baking soda
    2 tsp. baking powder
    3 eggs
    1 cup sweet milk
    1 tsp. vanilla
    About 5 cups flour
    12 ounces chocolate bits or chips

Preheat oven to 350°. Cream butter and sugar. Add eggs and vanilla. Add dry ingredients and milk alternately until dough is stiff. Add chocolate chips. Drop by the spoonful onto a greased cookie sheet. Bake 10–12 minutes at 350°. These cookies are best when topped with your favorite icing.

LISA'S PERSIMMON COOKIES
Indiana

I've never been to Indiana but have always known people from this state where Liz Taylor went "nuts" in the movie "Raintree County". I always asked these friends, where is Raintree County and is there really a raintree legend? They almost always say they're not aware of such a place or thing and most don't remember the movie either. Indiana does remember how to cook this American delight using persimmons. It's a "slap your mama" surprise taste for the holidays. Persimmons are common in the south and fresh ones are not hard to find.

    1 cup sugar
    ½ cup butter (1 stick)
    1 egg, beaten
    1 cup persimmon pulp
    1 T. baking soda, dissolved in pulp
    ½ T. cloves, nutmeg & cinnamon
    Dash of salt
    1 cup chopped nuts
    1 cup raisins
    2 cups flour

Cream sugar and butter. To this, add mixture of egg, pulp, soda and spices. Mix raisins, nuts and flour together, then add to pulp mixture. Drop onto greased cookie sheet and bake at 350° for about 10–12 minutes.

PERSIMMON PUDDING
Indiana

    2 cups persimmon pulp
    2 cups sugar
    2 eggs
    1 cup buttermilk
    1 tsp. baking soda
    ½ stick butter
    1¾ cup flour
    1 tsp. baking powder
    1 cup milk

Mix pulp, sugar and eggs. Add baking soda to buttermilk then add to the pulp mixture. Next add melted butter. Add baking powder to flour, then mix it in with the pulp, alternating with the milk. Pour mixture into a greased and floured baking pan or cake pan, and bake at 350° for 1 hour.

AUNT AGNES' SUGAR COOKIES
Arkansas

Ida Thompson of Tuna, Texas, provides us with her Aunt Agnes' old sugar cookie recipe. According to Ida, her aunt was the stingiest old woman in the world and never considered giving out her cookie recipe to the family. Ida claims the cookies were Aunt Agnes' insurance that she would always have visitors at the holidays. When Aunt Agnes passed on she left a will and in that will was the recipe willed to Ida herself. Ida cried and carried on for a week out of guilt. She had stolen Aunt Agnes' Sugar Cookie recipe years before when her Auntie "went in" for a corn removal.

  1 cup margarine
  1 cup vegetable oil
  1 cup sugar
  1 cup confectioners sugar
  2 eggs
  1 tsp. vanilla
  4 cups all-purpose flour
  1 tsp. salt
  1 tsp. baking soda
  1 tsp. cream of tartar

Cream margarine, oil, sugars and eggs, then add vanilla. In a separate bowl sift together flour, salt, soda and cream of tartar. Combine with the creamed mixture. Chill dough until firm, at least 1 hour.

To make into cookies, pinch off dough in small balls and place on a non-stick cookie sheet or a greased sheet pan. Flatten balls with tines of a fork that has been dipped in flour. Garnish each cookie with a pecan half, chocolate chips, red hot candies, or leave plain. Bake at 325° for 10–12 minutes or until brown. Makes 250 cookies.

BRUCE'S LAMINGTONS
Australia

Outback Bruce is famous in the Northern Territory of Australia for surviving a crocodile attack 15 years ago on the treacherous Daly River while out fishing with cousin Crocodile Mic Dundee.

Bruce: "Take your favorite sponge cake and cut it up into three or four-inch cubes. Heat your favorite cooking chocolate in a double boiler until fully melted. While chocolate is still warm, dip the cake cubes in, make sure they're coated on all sides. Allow excess chocolate to drip off, then dunk into a bowl of desiccated (dried) coconut, until fully covered. Then place the cake on your favorite serving dish and they're ready to eat. No worries, real simple and all your mates will love 'em."

To order additional copies of **Aunt Pearl's Cookbook,** please fill in the coupon below.

Mail to: **Pearl Productions**
Post Office Box 49301
Austin, Texas 78765

Please send me _____ copies of **Aunt Pearl's Cookbook** at $14.95 per copy, plus $2.00 postage and handling per book. Texas residents add 8% sales tax.

Enclosed is my check or money order for $___________.

(Please Print)

NAME____

ADDRESS ____

CITY________________ STATE________ ZIP____________

All profits from the sale of this cookbook go to AIDS research.

----------------------------------✀----------------------------------

To order additional copies of **Aunt Pearl's Cookbook,** please fill in the coupon below.

Mail to: **Pearl Productions**
Post Office Box 49301
Austin, Texas 78765

Please send me _____ copies of **Aunt Pearl's Cookbook** at $14.95 per copy, plus $2.00 postage and handling per book. Texas residents add 8% sales tax.

Enclosed is my check or money order for $___________.

(Please Print)

NAME____

ADDRESS ____

CITY________________ STATE________ ZIP____________

All profits from the sale of this cookbook go to AIDS research.